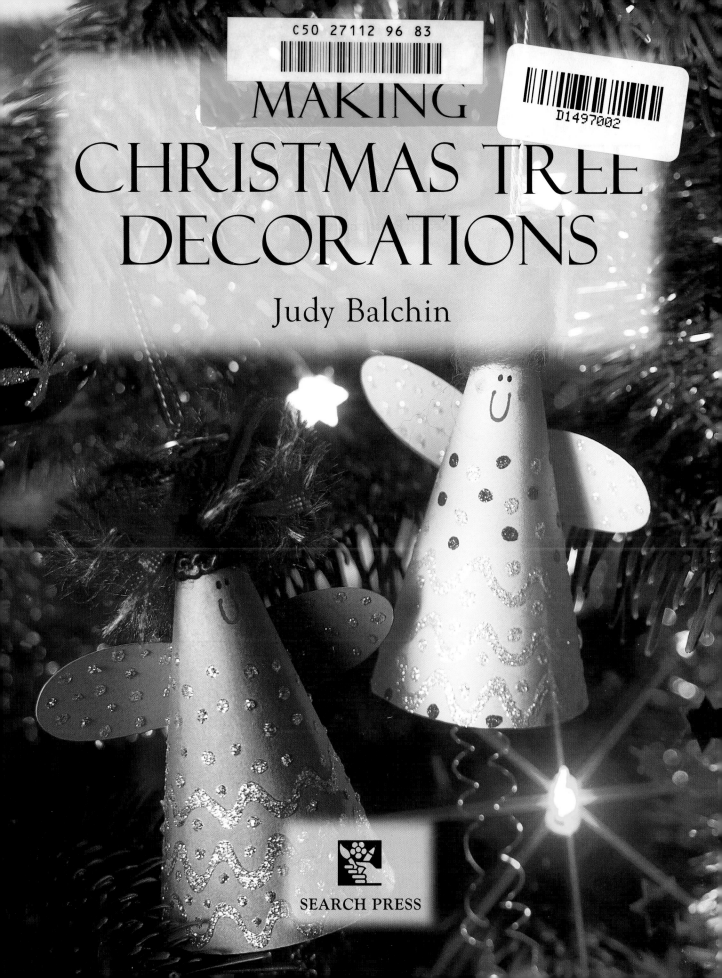

MAKING
CHRISTMAS TREE
DECORATIONS

Judy Balchin

SEARCH PRESS

First published in Great Britain 2006

Search Press Limited
Wellwood, North Farm Road,
Tunbridge Wells, Kent TN2 3DR

Text copyright © Judy Balchin 2006

Photographs by Roddy Paine Photographic Studios

Photographs and design copyright © Search Press Ltd. 2006

ISBN 978 1 84448 162 0

The Publishers and author can accept no responsibility for any
consequences arising from the information, advice or
instructions given in this publication.

Suppliers
If you have difficulty in obtaining any of the materials and
equipment mentioned in this book, then please visit the
Search Press website for details of suppliers:
www.searchpress.com

Publishers' note
All the step-by-step photographs in this book feature the
author, Judy Balchin, demonstrating how to make
Christmas tree decorations. No models have been used.

Printed in Malaysia by Times Offset (M) Sdn Bhd

Acknowledgements
*I would like to thank all the wonderfully
supportive people at Search Press for their help
and enthusiasm. Special thanks go to Editorial
Director Roz Dace for her continual guidance;
Edd Ralph for his hard work in editing the book;
Juan Hayward for his creative design skills and
Roddy Paine for his photography.*

Dedication
*To Briony and Des who always manage
to make Christmas 'rock'!*

Cover
*With a little card, paper, glitz and glitter, these Christmas
tree decorations are inexpensive and fun to create.*

Page 1
*These card angels are easy to make and fun to do. Use
different coloured card for each angel to really make them
stand out against the branches of your Christmas tree.*

Opposite
*Decorate papier-mâché gift boxes with paint, stickers and
jewels to make an extra-special tree gift.*

Contents

Introduction

Ah Christmas... It is my favourite time of year, so you can imagine what fun I've had making all these Christmas tree decorations. This book has been a joy to write and the projects seemed to almost create themselves in front of me. Christmas is a very special time spent with family and friends and preparations are usually in full swing well before the big day. Decorating the house is wonderful, but perhaps the crowning glory to any Christmas scene is the Christmas tree twinkling away. Be it a grand tree from floor to ceiling or a small one nestling in a corner, it just *has* to be decorated.

It was the husband of Queen Victoria, Prince Albert, who introduced the Christmas tree to this country in 1841, when he decorated the first tree at Windsor Castle with sweets, candles, gingerbread and fruit. In the 1850s, Charles Dickens describes a Christmas tree decorated with costume jewellery, toy guns, miniature furniture, musical instruments, fruits and sweets. It must have been magnificent to behold! By 1890 Christmas decorations were being imported from Germany. Nowadays, inexpensive shop-bought decorations are available everywhere. They are so much part of our Christmas experience that we can hardly imagine the time when they all had to be home-made. Now we have the choice, and hopefully by the time you have looked through the pages of this book, you will be inspired to have a go at making your own.

I have spent many hours in a haze of glitter and glue trying to give you a varied choice of decorations. We all have different tastes, but I am sure there will be something within these pages to tickle your fancy. Folk art garlands, funky angels, decorative crackers, festive tree present labels, sparkling stars and glitzy gift boxes are all waiting to be made and displayed on the big day.

So this gives you the perfect opportunity to enjoy those cosy nights in. Gather your family and a few friends, settle round that kitchen table and have some fun creating decorations for your own Christmas tree this year.

Judy

This picture shows just a small selection of the Christmas tree decorations in this book. All the decorations are inexpensive and fun to make.

Basic materials

You will not need all the materials shown here to start your projects. Each individual project has its own list of specific requirements.

General materials

A huge and wonderful range of card and backing papers are available in art and craft shops. This selection includes handmade papers, assorted coloured card and backing papers, metallic, pearlised, corrugated and holographic card and embossing foils. Papier-mâché blanks are available from art and craft shops in a wide variety of shapes and sizes.

Paints and inks

Acrylic paints are easily available from art and craft shops, as are inks. Use acrylic paints to sponge papier-mâché boxes before decorating. Coloured inks are used to paint watercolour paper. Glitter glue is great for bringing a little sparkle to your Christmas tree decorations.

Stamps and embossing powders

Rubber stamps, embossing pads and powders are available from art and craft outlets. Look out for Christmas themed stamps for your decorations. The heating tool is used to melt the embossing powder on to a surface. Take care with the heating tool, as it is extremely hot, and be sure to work on a heatproof surface.

Embellishments

Ribbons, embroidery thread, wire, cord, raffia, fancy yarns, beads, buttons, sequins, craft jewels, mini pegs, paper stars, eyelets, craft stickers – the list goes on. All can be used to enhance your Christmas tree decorations.

Other materials and equipment

Pencil Use this to trace round templates or copy them on to card or paper.

Ruler For measuring card, drawing straight lines and, with the back of a scalpel, to score a fold.

Fine black felt tip pen To draw round the painted star template and to add stitch lines to punched motifs.

Pencil crayon Use this to draw the mouth and cheeks on to the angel cone.

Paintbrushes Use a large brush to apply water and coloured inks to watercolour paper. Use the rounded end of a paintbrush to emboss foil.

Old ballpoint pen Use this for embossing foil.

Palette Squeeze paint on to a palette when using a sponge to decorate an item.

Scalpel Use this to cut card and to score a fold with the back of the scalpel.

Cutting mat Use a cutting mat when cutting card or paper with a scalpel.

Needle Use to thread ribbons, buttons and sequins.

Scissors Trim ribbon and thread with scissors.

Old scissors Use old scissors to cut wire.

Old notepad To use when embossing foils.

Masking tape Use to secure a pattern to foil when embossing.

Spray glue For securing card or paper to surfaces.

Clear glue Use to attach craft jewels and buttons.

Glue line A strong line of glue used to secure the cracker and the angel cone.

Sponge Papier-mâché boxes are sponged with paint to give an even, slightly textured surface.

Hairdryer Use to speed up the drying of paper painted with coloured inks.

Eyelet kit This includes a hammer and mat, and a multipurpose tool for punching holes in card and paper and setting eyelets.

Plastic tubing Use to roll the paper when making a Christmas cracker.

String Use to create the indentations in a Christmas cracker and to string together a garland.

Punches Use to cut paper shapes for decoration.

SEASONAL STOCKING GARLAND

You will need

Red and green handmade papers

Watercolour paper

Fine black felt tip pen

Paper stars

Heart punch

String

Raffia

Mini pegs

Glitter glue

Clear glue

Pencil

Scissors

As a child I can well remember the enjoyment of making brightly coloured paper garlands for the Christmas tree. With a little paper, string, and glitter glue it is amazing what you can come up with! These mini stocking garlands are easy and fun to make. Keep the basic shapes simple as you will be cutting out quite a few to create your garland. The stitching adds a folk art feel and is done quickly and easily with a felt tip pen.

The templates for the Seasonal Stocking Garland project, reproduced at actual size.

1. Photocopy the stocking template and cut it out. Lay it on handmade paper and draw round it with a pencil. Make four stockings of each colour.

2. Cut out the stockings.

3. Punch eight hearts; four of each colour.

4. Use the cuff template to help you make the eight cuffs. Tear 5mm (¼in) from each edge. Glue the cuffs to the tops of the stockings using clear glue.

11

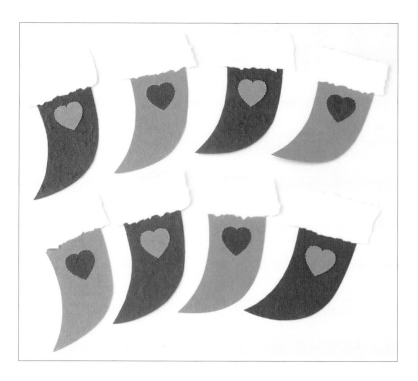

5. Attach the hearts in alternating colours on to the stocking using clear glue.

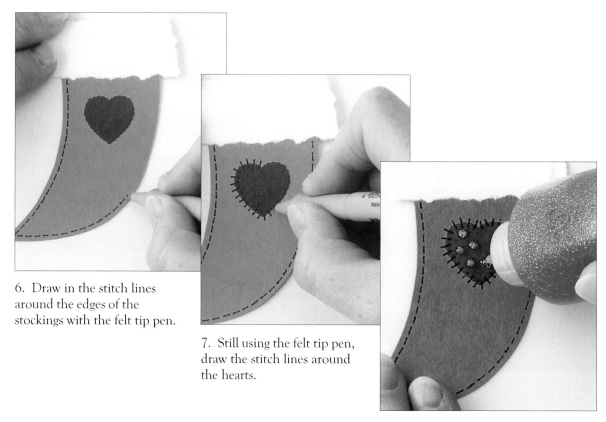

6. Draw in the stitch lines around the edges of the stockings with the felt tip pen.

7. Still using the felt tip pen, draw the stitch lines around the hearts.

8. Decorate the hearts with dots of glitter glue.

9. Run a line of glitter glue down the front of eight mini pegs.

10. Tie small raffia bows down a length of string.

Tip

Traditional colours are used to create this garland. As an alternative, try using more unusual colour combinations for a more modern look.

11. Peg the stockings and a paper star between each bow, with the glittery side of the peg to the front.

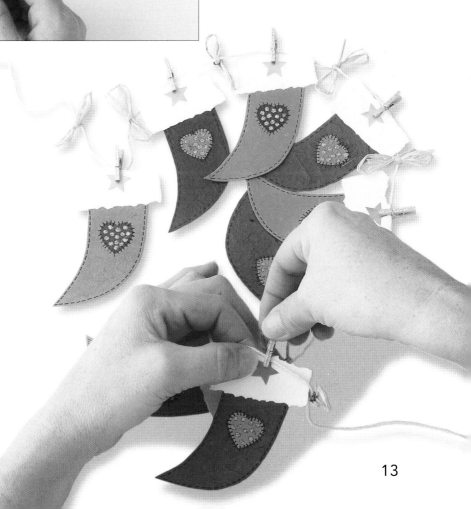

13

This garland is simple to make but very effective when strung across the tree branches.

Simple shapes, textured papers and a little glitter glue are used to create these garlands.

FLIGHTS OF FANCY

This basic cone shape gives you great scope for decoration. Have fun creating a host of twinkling angels to fly through the branches of your Christmas tree. Use bright coloured fancy yarns to give them funky hairstyles to match their glitzy robes and beaded feet.

You will need

White card, 13 x 18cm (5 x 7in)

Pink card, 4 x 10cm (1½ x 4in)

Iridescent glitter glue

Black felt tip pen

Pink pencil crayon

Silver wire

Pink beads

Pink fancy yarn

Pink embroidery thread

Pencil

Paintbrush

Ruler

Scissors

Scalpel

Cutting mat

Glue line

Clear glue

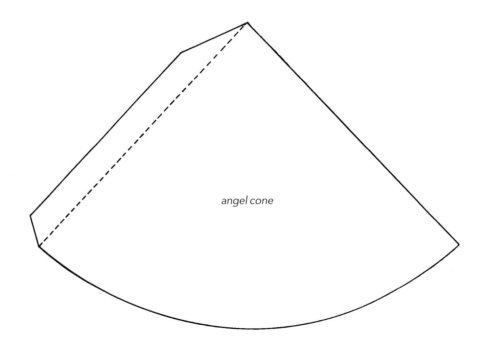

angel cone

wings

The templates for the Flights of Fancy project, reproduced at three quarters of the actual size. Enlarge them to 133 per cent on a photocopier.

1. Lay the angel template on to the white card, and the wings template on to the pink card. Draw round them and cut them out.

2. Score down the inner line of the angel cone with the back of the scalpel, using the dotted line on the template to help you with positioning.

3. Draw in the eyes with a felt tip pen. Draw in the mouth with a pencil crayon and colour in the cheeks.

4. Pipe swirls of glitter glue over the body area of the angel and leave to dry.

Tip

As an alternative, try piping spots, stars or stripes of glitter glue on to the cone.

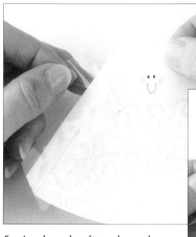

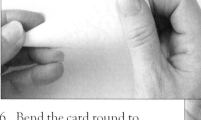

5. Apply a glue line along the tab of the angel cone and peel off the backing paper.

6. Bend the card round to create the cone shape, securing it with the glue line.

7. Make a loop in the middle of a 60cm (24in) piece of wire. Twist the loop round to form a secure hoop.

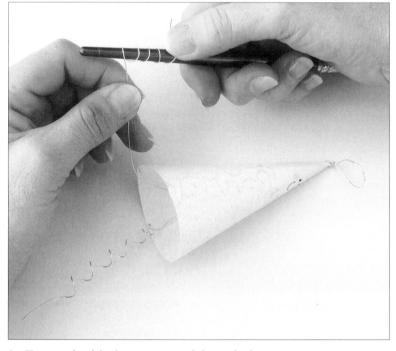

8. Poke the ends of the wire down through the top of the cone to create the legs, then bend the hoop over to create the halo.

9. Twist each of the leg wires round the end of a paintbrush to create spirals.

10. Thread a bead on to the end of each spiral. Bend the wires back and twist to secure.

Tip

The angel's hair can be created with coloured wool, pipe cleaners, raffia or string. The choice is yours!

11. Apply clear glue to the top of the cone and wrap with fancy yarn.

12. Use clear glue to attach the wings to the back of the angel.

13. Tie a loop of matching embroidery thread to the wire halo for the hanger.

There is always room for humour and these angels will certainly raise a smile.

Make a host of different angels by using different coloured yarns for hair and fancy card for the wings.

LABELS OF LOVE

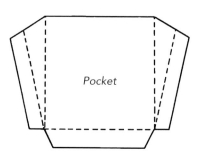

You will need

A5 sheet of red card

Music-themed backing paper, 6 x 6 cm (2¼ x 2¼in)

Floral backing paper, 6 x 6cm (2¼ x 2¼in)

Gold embossing foil

Ballpoint pen

Paintbrush

Old notepad

Gold star and line craft stickers

Eyelet kit

Gold eyelet

Gold cord

Clear glue

Spray glue

Pencil

Scissors

Ruler

Scalpel

Cutting mat

Masking tape

Many of us hang small 'tree presents' on the tree at Christmas. These are personal gifts especially for those sharing the festive Christmas celebrations. This decorative label is ideal as it provides you with a small pocket to hold the gift. The pocket is decorated with an embossed initial to personalise the label and make it something to treasure.

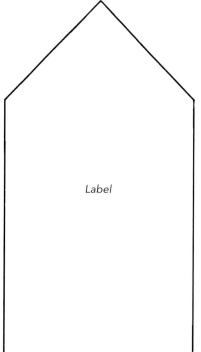

Label

The templates for the Labels of Love project, reproduced at three quarters of the actual size. Enlarge them to 133 per cent on a photocopier.

Pocket

1. Cut out a label and pocket shape from card using the templates to help you.

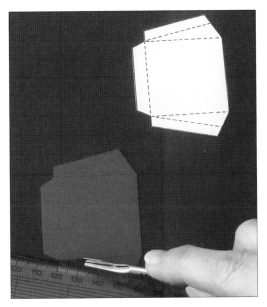

2. Score the lines on the pocket with the back of the scalpel.

3. Tear a 5mm (¼in) strip from the left-hand side of the music backing paper and spray glue it to the label.

4. Turn the label over and trim off the excess paper.

5. Tear a 5mm (¼in) strip from the right-hand edge of the floral backing and glue it in place.

6. Photocopy the required letter from the alphabet (see pages 46–47 for further templates). Cut round it and tape it to the back of the gold embossing foil.

7. Lay the foil on a padded surface. Trace over the design with a ballpoint pen.

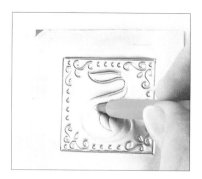

8. Remove the pattern and trace over it once more to deepen the embossed line.

9. Use the rounded end of a paintbrush to emboss the letter.

10. Fold the pocket flaps back. Spread the flaps with clear glue and press the pocket on to the label.

11. Cut out the letter square and glue it to the front of the pocket.

12. Decorate the label with star and line craft stickers.

13. Punch a hole in the top of the label with the hole punch and hammer.

14. Insert an eyelet and hammer the back with the eyelet setter to secure.

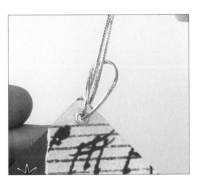

15. Thread the hole with cord, creating a half-hitch as shown.

16. Tie the cord in a knot at the top to create the hanger.

17. Wrap a small gift in festive paper and slip it into the pocket.

The embossed gold foil and craft stickers add an extra sparkle to this festive label.

Use bells, craft jewels, craft stickers and assorted backing papers to create labels for all your family and friends.

WHAT A CRACKER!

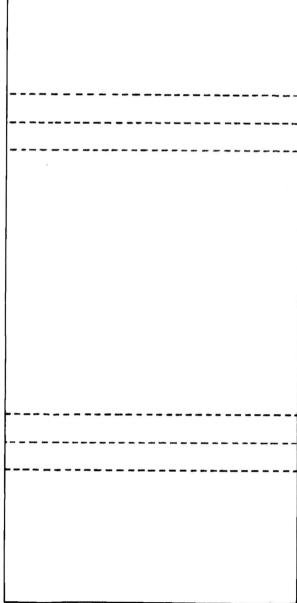

You will need

Floral backing paper,
8 x 17cm (3 x 6¾in)

Gold paper, A5

Gold wire

Pink ribbon,
50cm (20in)

Button

Length of plastic
tubing, approximate
diameter 2cm (¾in)

Glue line

Spray glue

Old scissors

Scalpel

Cutting mat

Ruler and pencil

String

No Christmas tree is complete without a few Christmas crackers. This basic cracker is created using background paper and decorated with gold paper, wire and a button to give a delicate feminine look. You could choose to use bolder coloured background paper and embellishments to create a more traditional look to your crackers.

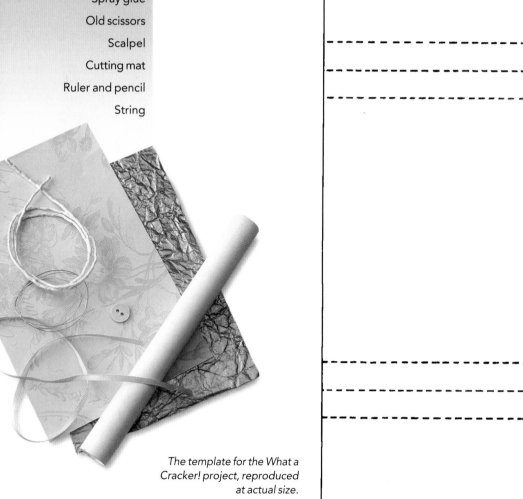

The template for the What a Cracker! project, reproduced at actual size.

1. Using the dotted lines on the template to help you with positioning, draw six lines across the back of the background paper.

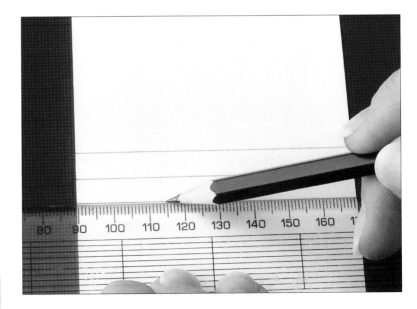

Tip

For larger crackers, enlarge the template and use a thicker length of plastic tubing.

2. With the back of the scalpel, lightly score the six lines on the cracker.

3. Cut slits between the scored lines as shown.

4. Turn the backing paper over and spray glue a 2cm (¾in) wide strip of gold paper across the end of the cracker. Then tear a 5mm (¼in) strip from the end of the cracker.

5. Repeat this process on the other end of the cracker.

6. Apply a glue line to one edge of the back of the paper. Place the tube along the opposite edge and roll the paper round the tube.

7. Remove the tube. Wrap a length of string around the middle scored line at one end of the cracker and pull to tighten. Repeat with the other end of the cracker.

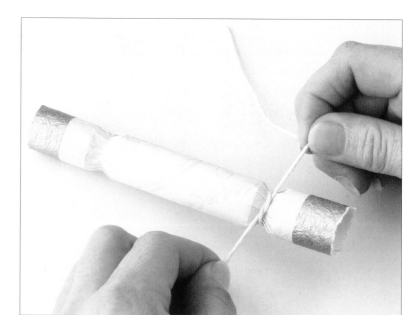

8. Remove the string and wrap the indentations with wire. Twist the ends of the wires together to secure and trim to neaten.

9. Cut a 5.5 x 7cm (2 x 2¾in) piece of gold paper and tear 5mm (¼in) from each edge. Use spray glue to attach it to the barrel of the cracker.

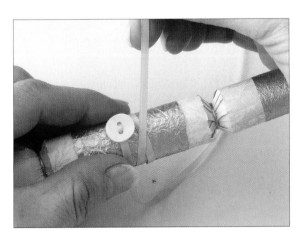

10. Thread a button on to the middle of the ribbon and wrap the ribbon around the cracker.

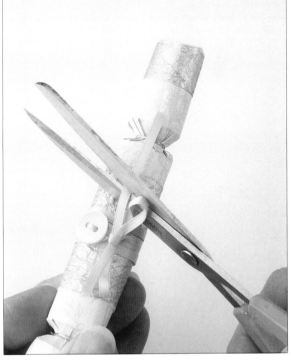

11. Tie the ribbon in a bow and trim the ends to neaten.

Using pastel coloured backing paper to create the cracker gives it a Victorian feel.

Opposite
Sprinkle your tree with assorted crackers created with different backing papers and embellishments.

STAR OF WONDER

You will need

A4 sheet of heavy watercolour paper

Coloured inks: magenta, cyan and violet

Star rubber stamp

Clear embossing pad

Gold embossing powder

Paintbrush

Gold card, 14cm x 14cm (5½ x 5½in)

Gold wire

Eyelet kit and hammer

Six gold eyelets

Black felt tip pen

Spray glue

Scalpel and cutting mat

Old scissors

Hairdryer

Heating tool

If, like me, you love playing and experimenting with colour and texture, then this project is for you. Have fun merging the coloured inks on watercolour paper to create your basic star. Then let fly with the stamp and embossing powder before lacing your star with wire for that final flourish.

The template for the Star of Wonder project, reproduced at actual size.

1. Draw a 13cm (5in) square on to the middle of a piece of watercolour paper and paint it generously with water.

2. Spot the square with the magenta ink, letting the colour bleed across the damp surface.

3. While the square is still damp, spot the other inks on to the paper, letting them blend into each other until the whole surface is covered.

Tip
You can use a hairdryer to speed up the drying process.

5. Sprinkle the square with embossing powder.

4. Allow to dry. Press the star stamp into a clear embossing pad and stamp all over the square.

6. Shake off the excess powder and heat with a heating tool.

7. Photocopy and cut out the star template. Lay it on the painted square and draw round it with a felt tip pen. Cut it out.

Tip

Remember to use the heating tool on a heatproof surface.

8. Spray glue the star to gold card and cut round it, leaving a small gold border.

9. Punch five holes round the inner points of the star and one at the top of the star.

10. Insert gold eyelets into the holes, turn the star over and hammer each eyelet with the setting tool.

11. Bring the wire up through one of the inner point eyelets, and working clockwise, take it down two eyelets further on. Still working clockwise, bring the wire up one eyelet further on, as shown.

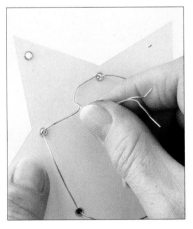

12. Continue threading the wire until you have a wire star on the front as shown. The wire should form a pentagon shape on the back of the star.

13. Twist the ends of the wire together at the back and trim.

14. Thread the top hole with wire, and spiral the wire ends around a paintbrush.

15. Finally, twist the wire ends together to create the hanger.

The pink and blue colouring of this decoration stands out well from the dark green foliage.

*Emboss your basic stars with different stamps and powders
and try lacing them with ribbons.*

GLITZY GIFT BOX

You will need

Papier-mâché box

White acrylic paint

Sheet of gold craft stickers

Sponge

Palette

Needle

White embroidery thread

Decorative large gold sequin

Gold beads

Faceted craft jewels

Ribbon, 70cm (27½in)

Clear glue

Scissors

Scalpel

These small papier-mâché boxes make unusual but attractive Christmas tree decorations. The box is sponged with acrylic paint to give an even, textured surface. A gift can be slipped into the box before assembling.

1. Sponge the lid and base of the box with white paint and leave to dry.

2. Apply a gold craft sticker to each facet of the lid.

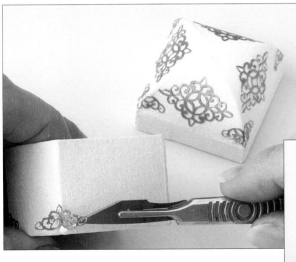

3. Apply the corner stickers to the lid and base.

4. Make a hole in the top of the lid with a needle.

5. Thread the needle with two lengths of embroidery thread and knot the end. Push the needle up through the hole.

6. Thread it through the two lengths of ribbon.

7. Thread the decorative sequin.

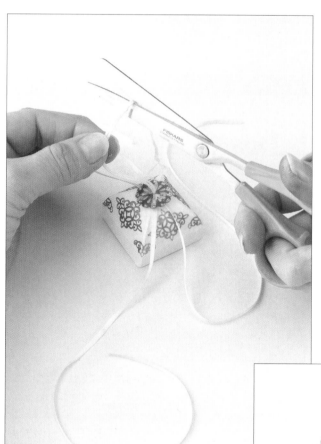

8. Remove the needle, tie the thread in a knot and trim the thread.

9. Insert your gift and put the lid on the base. Pull the ribbons down over the sides of the box and thread the ends through a bead.

10. Tie a knot in the ribbons to secure the bead. Trim the ribbons.

11. Cut each ribbon lengthwise to create a tassel.

12. Glue a craft jewel to each facet of the lid.

These mini papier-mâché boxes are perfect for decorating and hanging on your tree.

Paint your boxes with traditional or funky colours – the choice is yours!

Templates

Use the alphabet templates and the heart and star templates for the Labels of Love project on pages 22–27. The heart, star and triangle templates can also be used to make Christmas tree garlands, following the instructions on pages 10–15.